# HOT ROD RACING

## THE GOLDEN YEARS

# HOT ROD RACING

## THE GOLDEN YEARS

RICHARD JOHN NEIL

TEMPUS

*Frontispiece:* The ever-popular Mick Collard looks justifiably happy after winning the BP Series final at Wimbledon in 1979. 'Duffy' had a successful year, also winning the Grand Prix Series.

First published 2004

Tempus Publishing Limited
The Mill, Brimscombe Port,
Stroud, Gloucestershire, GL5 2QG
www.tempus-publishing.com



British Library Cataloguing in Publication Data.
A catalogue record for this book is available from the British Library.

ISBN 0 7524 3241 9

Typesetting and origination by Tempus Publishing Limited.
Printed in Great Britain.

# Contents

# Acknowledgements

Massive thanks to Andy Weltch for his encouragement with this project. If you enjoyed this book then I would highly recommend his own books, also published by Tempus. Thanks also to Glenn Burtenshaw, Fred Buss, Robin Clark, Neil Clarke, Martin Davey, John Duhig, Peter Freestone, Sonny and Barbara Howard, Alan Humphrey, Dave and Carole Longhurst, Mac McCormack, David, Wendy, Jamie and Leah Oates, George Rimmer, The Eric Setchell Collection, Ez Walker and Jim Whitehouse. I would never have started this project if it hadn't been for my parents, David and June Neil, getting me hooked on the whole motorsport thing in the first place – thanks folks! Also, I would never have completed it without the support of my lovely wife, Michele (yes, I'm off the PC now – cuppa splosh?).

# Introduction

Hot rod racing was born during Easter 1963, when three cars took part in a demonstration race at Hednesford Hills raceway in Staffordshire. The class was seen as an alternative to the crash-and-bash racing provided for over a decade before by the stock cars. The three-car debut was hardly a huge success but Bill Morris, the man behind the formula, was sure that the style of racing he had seen on his visits to the USA would eventually catch on. He was proved right and over the next few years there was clearly a market for non-contact saloon car racing on the quarter-mile stock car (often speedway) tracks. This was evidenced by the large crowds who would watch their heroes in action every week. Hot rod racing was unlike anything the race fans had seen before – there would be fields of up to thirty cars, with the best drivers having to start each race at the back of the grid and battle their way through the pack without the aid of the front bumper to remove the opposition! The Ford Anglia was the car to have at the start of the 1970s but it was soon challenged by the Escort and frequently upset by the enduring Mini.

Non-contact racing developed at a considerable pace throughout the late 1960s and early 1970s. International interest began in the early 1970s with the first World Championship race being contested in 1972. Inter-promotional team races and international test series were also contested as the formula fulfilled its potential. In 1978 the UK's promoters got together and set up the forerunner of today's 'national' formula, the Grand Prix Series. Each promoter entered its top drivers into an elite group that toured the UK, battling it out on average once every two weeks throughout the season.

As preparation standards increased, so costs went up. Alternative classes were then introduced to encourage new drivers onto the circuits. The 1300cc stock rod formula and the 2.5-litre minimum super rods were two such classes, but the hot rods remained the cars that the fans flocked to see.

Some 1966 Hot Rod action at the formula's home circuit, Hednesford. Bill Kay's Standard 10 (no. 18) spins onto the infield.

For me, several factors made the racing so good. First and foremost was having the best drivers starting at the back of the grid. Giving newcomers (or maybe those without the right equipment, ability or luck) the sporting chance of a win from a generous grid position often provided a pleasant surprise and encouraged many a new driver to persevere with racing until he reached the top end of the points table. Reversed grids still provide the best action for any form of motorsport and many people agree that it is an admission that something is wrong with the specifications when the top drivers don't start at the back. Secondly there were the characters, some of whom I have had the pleasure to get to know over the years. Racing today still has its characters and true sportsmen, but perhaps they are not as well promoted and certainly the racing is not watched by as many people as the era this book looks at.

In truth, there is no definite start or finishing point for the golden era of hot rod racing, as the 1980s and 1990s also produced some great racing, colourful characters and superb machinery. However, space is finite, and so this volume looks only at images of the sport from the 1970s. It is fair to say that I've just scratched the surface – there are many, many more drivers who could feature in a second volume.

one

# 1971–1973

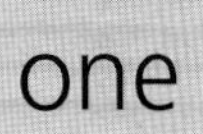

For many this captures the essence of classic hot rod racing – 1971 under the floodlights at Wimbledon. Barry Lee (nearest camera) is in the 351 Emmins Spares Escort with George Polley trying to nip up the inside in his BP/*Custom Car* magazine-backed Anglia.

Ex-stock car racer Dave Bozzard made the switch to hot rods early on. This is his 1971 Escort captured in action at Wimbledon Stadium.

George Polley looks rather pleased with himself, although we can only guess why he's receiving a gift-wrapped offering rather than the customary trophy from commentator Nigel King.

The 'Cockney Whizz Kid' Graham North (267) leads Midlands visitor Brian Pedley (9) and George Polley at Wimbledon in 1971. Pedley was a frequent traveller to the southern circuits and bagged third place in the British Championship each year from 1969 to 1971.

Barry Lee takes the outside line around white-top racer Mike Powrie (311) at Wimbledon. Lee's history is well documented; Powrie made it to Spedeworth Blue Grade by 1974.

Gilbert Sills (53) leads Tony Brown at Hednesford in an early Spedeworth *v.* Hednesford team match.

Bill Wilcox (214) chased by Brian Vawer (7). Vawer came to hot rods after racing motorcycles and was one of the first UK short-oval drivers to compete in America.

This photograph is typical of the action that attracted fans in their thousands to hot rod racing at Hednesford in the early 1970s. Bill Edwards (222) is well out of the way of the trouble involving Roger Webster (169) and Steve Gately.

*Above:* Twice National Champion (1971 and 1972) Ron Higgins at speed at Hednesford in 1971. Higgins started racing in the economy car class in 1966 and retired from hot rods about a year later.

*Opposite above:* Steve Gately (178) in action in 1971. Steve was runner up in the 1969 National Championship but was disqualified along with race winner Terry Haywood for running an oversized engine. Both drivers' engines measured identically on race day but Haywood demanded a recheck the following day as he felt the first one had been done incorrectly. On the recheck Haywood's engine was within the legal 1703cc limit and he was reinstated. Gately did not avail himself of a second check and lost his place as runner up.

*Opposite below:* Barry Kibble was the 1966 National Champion and runner up in the years either side. 1966 was the last year the title was awarded to the top points scorer as opposed to the winner of a single championship race.

178

STP
Sponsored By
H
55
Autosales of Bilston

*Above:* Barry Lee (351), Barry Kibble (55) and Roger Webster (169) dice in the 1971 National Championship.

*Opposite above:* Dave Wilde's (71) Mini sports an interesting Clubman-style front end. He is racing here with Barry Kibble (55), with Ron Higgins just nosing into shot.

*Opposite below:* A unique event each year in the Spedeworth calendar was 'Carnival Night' where, to celebrate the end of each season, cars were decorated as floats for the grand parade. Eddie Asling played on his racing number (553) and emerged as 'Herbie the Lovebug' for this event. If you look closely you can make out his Ford Anglia nestling underneath the disguise.

EAST
BEND
DUNLOP
71
sales of Bilston

Herbie
553

*Above:* Hot rod racing was growing in popularity not only in the UK but also overseas. Denmark was one of the first countries to run this type of racing and a Danish touring side was assembled to compete against the English in 1971. This action, shot from Denmark's shale Korskrobanen, shows three NSU TTs battling it out.

Trouble on the back straight at Arlington. Gordon Streeter (151) faces the wrong way while Peter Ruse (4) tries to squeeze through on the outside. Stephen Cann (82) is followed by Frank Hartley (178)

Paul Smyth came into hot rod racing after a spell in rallycross and raced in the class for four seasons, three of which were in the colours of BP Oils and *Custom Car* magazine. He was one of the few drivers to attain and hold the lead in the points chart while campaigning in a Mini. He is seen here in a team race against the Danish touring side in 1972 – hence his racing anti-clockwise. Paul retired from the sport in 1974 and he has two grown-up sons who compete successfully in motocross.

19
166

*Above:* The BP/*Custom Car* team clearly went for quality as well as quantity. George Polley's Anglia was actually the first hot rod to sport the team colours.

*Opposite:* Mick Collard's 1972 Escort (foreground) featured in a multi-formula feature in *Custom Car* magazine. His car came up for comparison against (from the top) a rally car, a drag race version and a circuit racer.

H64
306
KEITH PIERCE · DEREK FINCH
H64
WELLER
CUSTOM CAR
MAGAZINE
BP

00

*Above:* Spedeworth *v*. Hednesford team racing at Wimbledon in 1972. The London stadium has always been a good place to watch racing and the scoreboard clearly shows the race positions before this contretemps. Brian Vawer (7) nips through on the inside of Al Leeson (189) with Barry Lee and Dave Bozzard taking to the inner speedway circuit to avoid the mêlée.

*Opposite above:* BP/*Custom Car* teammates Paul Smyth and a rather manic-looking George Polley line up against each other prior to a race at Ipswich in 1972.

*Opposite below:* The first ever hot rod driver was Martin Morris, who therefore gained the 00 racing number. The twice National Champion (1964 and 1967) is pictured here in the latter days of his hot rod racing. He went on to race a Capri 'Speedcar' in the colours of *Auto* magazine.

71
222

111
111

*Above:* It looks like time for a stoppage in the racing at Hednesford Hills. Norman Humphries (04) attempts to mate with Brian Pedley's Mini while an unidentified and somewhat undignified car does a good job of blocking the circuit.

*Opposite above:* Bill Edwards (222) leads David Wilde (71) at Hednesford in 1972.

*Opposite below:* Fire in the boot! Hednesford Mini man Ken Deakin finds the going a little hot and the marshals prove invaluable as ever. Note the attendant nearest the driver with the cigarette. No problem since the car is already on fire!

Ready for the off at Wimbledon Stadium. George Polley in the colours of BP/*Custom Car* is set to chase through the field. Ahead of him is another Anglia, that of his former mechanic, Phil 'Squeaker' Powell.

Malcolm Ford looks determined at the wheel of his battle-scarred Anglia (Hednesford 1972).

A crowded pit area at Foxhall Heath, Ipswich. The Anglias nearest the camera are Melvyn Smith (228) and Dave Bye (37). Smith was third in the World Championship that year. Also present are Noddy Robinson (432), Gordon Scott (377), Butch Murton (12) and Bob Wilson (92).

Racing would not be possible without the services of the St John Ambulance. Receiving attention here is Frank Hartley, who has suffered a rather nasty collision with the Ipswich safety fence.

Alan Bee ran the eponymous 'Beespeed' outfit and was the teammate of 1972 World Champion Bob Howe. Three cars ran under the Beespeed banner, under the number sequence of 108 (Bob Howe), 208 (Bee) and 308 (Dick Flack). Just behind Alan's car is a yellow-graded Leon Smith in 401.

*Above:* Jeff Cushing (75) battles with Melvyn Smith (228) and the Mk1 Cortina of Ray Codling (536).

*Opposite below:* More of the line-up for the grid draw prior to the 1972 World Championship. On the right of the picture you can just see the front of Danish driver Steen Gudmansen's Mini. To the left of him is top Midlands man Ken Deakin with Bob Howe and Pete Woodward next along.

These days drivers have to score points all year to determine their grid position for the World Championship, with the top scorers securing the front positions. Back in 1972 for the first ever World Championship things were a little different, with positions being drawn by ballot. Eventual winner Bob Howe is pictured here awaiting the grid draw for the big race.

Ken Deakin is in trouble again as he gets it sideways across the front of Gordon Scott with John Kirk on the inside. Jan Murray's car (95) is already in the fence!

Scotsman Malcolm Watt (130) is chased by George Polley (306) with Danish Champion Arnold Larsen taking the outside line in his Renault.

A Ford Anglia battle at Ipswich in 1972, as Graham North (267) battles with Derek Green (6). North's car sports the colours of *Auto Enthusiast* magazine, while Green would have to wait until the following season to race in the colours of rival publication *Custom Car*.

Kingston's Peter Ruse (4) battles his way through a pack of Anglias and a Cortina at Ipswich in 1972.

DIAGRIT ELECTROMETALLICS
ARCO

*Above:* The early days of the Production Car formula at Newton Abbot, 22 October 1972. Uniquely in this formula the cars were identified by letters rather than race numbers. Minis in varying forms were popular – a Mini Pick-up (Q) leads a Mini-van, a Riley Elf and a conventional model!

*Opposite above:* Malcolm Smith (84) pursuing a group of cars headed by Kent man Charlie Brown (73). Smith was and still is one of the best engine builders in the business.

*Opposite below:* Dave Smart (335) leads Scotsman Ian Bruce's Mini at Ipswich. Bruce retired from the sport not long after this but made a successful comeback in the early 1980s.

*Above:* Mick Collard's Escorts were always immaculate and he formed part of the BP/*Custom Car* team in 1973. This shot was taken on his farm shortly after the completion of his new challenger.

*Opposite above:* John Duhig's Ford Consul Classic 315 picked out at a wet Aldershot meeting. This was the first of three cars that John raced. 'Too heavy, but superb handling,' he says now. 'I wanted to be "different" from all the Escorts.'

*Opposite below: Custom Car* found themselves with some competition in 1973 when *Auto* magazine supported a number of drivers in various formulae. Hot rods were well supported with Ken Deakin sporting their colours at Hednesford, Leon Smith (pictured here in action at Ipswich) at Spedeworth and the Freestone brothers, Martin and Peter down in the West Country.

H 406
H 406

BROADSPEED
auto

Martin Freestone enjoyed his best year in the sport in 1974 taking second place in the European Championship at Kaldenkirchen behind Barry Lee.

Ken Deakin was one of the original three hot rod drivers and a very quick driver. This is his immaculate 1973 car ready for action at Hednesford.

Barry Lee at speed around Aldershot in 1973.

Where would the top drivers have been without the white graders? Here is Paul Turner of Middleton-on-Sea in his smart Anglia at Aldershot in 1973.

David Humphrey (62) and Dave Taylor (70) battle it out at Aldershot on 20 April 1973. David's Spedeworth statement suggests that he got a third place at the meeting. He went on to be top Blue Grade later that year but missed the elusive Red Grade by just a handful of points. He represented Spedeworth at Hednesford later that year when they beat the Midland Hot Rod Club.

Surrey-based racer Pete Chambers (80) went on to become a top circuit racer – a treble champion in the Porsche Cup. Pete also had the distinction of winning the first ever Pickup Truck race at Brands Hatch in 1997. He is pictured here in his smart Mk1 Escort at his local circuit, Aldershot Stadium, back in 1973, dicing with Barry Lee (351) and Pete Gatehouse (190), with Roger Homer (Mini) just nosing into view.

South Coast-based driver Roger Homer at speed in his immaculate Mini at Aldershot Stadium in 1973.

Dick Armiger (16) in action at Aldershot raceway. Escorts were increasing in numbers – Tony Marren's smart 102 machine is pictured on the outside line.

*Above:* Hardly roadworthy… Derek Green's battle-scarred Escort is seen parked up, presumably near his Camberwell base in South London. 1973 was the first of his two seasons with the BP/*Custom Car* team.

*Opposite above:* The Ford 100E was the UK's best-selling car in the mid-1950s and so there were plenty around to use as hot rods for some years. This one, raced by William Clough in 1973 at Hednesford, is possibly the last one of its type to grace the small ovals.

*Opposite below:* Spedeworth driver Pete Gatehouse travelled widely during his career and is pictured here at Hednesford during a team meeting. The Farnborough-based driver was a consistent front runner despite using a pre-crossflow engine after they went out of fashion with many of the other top drivers. He was introduced to the sport by Al Leeson but retired after a few seasons to concentrate on his business.

727
610
KENILWORTH AUTOS
M 33

190
BP 190

Dave Riley was a leading light in Modern Stock Cars, who made the move into hot rods. His brief career consisted of a handful of meetings with several wins before this visit to the fence at Brafield.

Paul Storr in the pits at Hednesford during an inter-promotional team meeting. At the back of the picture on the right-hand side is Barry Lee's ex-works transporter.

The unusual Wolseley of Derek Caunce made it into the Blue Grade at Hednesford. An early Gordon Bland Escort is seen challenging on the outside line.

Midland Hot Rod Club action at Northampton. Lol Winter's unusual Renault spins out of contention.

TOM LAFFEY RACING
racing
121
CORPORATION ST.
SERVICE
STATION B'HAM
Tom
Laffey
Esso

WYNN'S
WEBSTER
ALMERS GARAGE
Cradley Heath
169
GOODYEAR

*Above:* Multiple Danish Champion Arnold Larsen (2) battles with South African racer Bobby Scott (85) in the 1973 World Championship at Ipswich. Scott used a borrowed Ford Anglia for the meeting and, unlike the Danes, had the advantage of right-hand drive. Scott finished fourth in 1972 and fifth in 1973. Scott went on to race Formula Ford and came up against ex-Superstox World Champion and one time hot-rodder Derek Warwick in 1976. The South Africans continued to send effective opposition to the World Championship and took fourth again in 1975 through Happy Steenkamp.

*Opposite above:* The Midlands drivers were no slouches at car preparation – Tom Laffey's immaculate Team Uniflow Escort set the style standard and the race pace at Hednesford.

*Opposite below:* Midlands star Roger Webster with the chequered flag.

*Left:* Carl-Erik Kristensen was a prolific visitor during the early to mid-1970s. As a Danish rallycross and special saloon champion, his pedigree was never in doubt. Thirty years on, both his sons are also quick racing drivers. His eldest son, Tom, has won Le Mans six times while his younger son, Jacob, is a successful touring-car racer in Denmark.

*Below:* Alan Humphrey's hot rod debut at Arlington, 11 August 1973. He had declined Spedeworth's request to make his debut in the formula for the promoter's team in an away team match at Hednesford (his brother David, an established hot rod racer, was in the team).

Peter Freestone takes part in the Grand Parade prior to the 1973 World Championship.

Avengers were few and far between, but Maurice Smith raced this smart example with an Imp for back-up!

The 1973 line-up from Wimbledon Stadium. Cars under the floodlights on the back straight include Micky Codling's Anglia (566). Next to him is Leon Smith with Malcolm Goodman and Dave Bozzard on the row in front.

East Londoner Geoff Cowley at speed around the Plough Lane bend at Wimbledon Stadium. He made it to Star Grade driving a more conventional Escort but was not afraid to experiment with other models, as this picture shows.

Malcolm Goodman awaits the off under the floodlights at Wimbledon Stadium in 1972. Goodman went on to become a multiple champion in Grand Prix Midgets during the late 1970s and early 1980s but not before winning the English Championship in hot rods in 1973.

Alan 'Noddy' Robinson (432) also enjoyed a successful career in stock cars. Here he leads Leon Smith at Wimbledon in 1973.

Pete Woodward (129) was one of only a handful of drivers to race a Ford Capri. He managed to bag a few race wins as well. Alan Humphrey (162) has the edge on him here, with Barry Lee (351) in hot pursuit at Wimbledon in November 1973.

One of the few Ford Capris to be raced back in 1973, this one belonging to Gerry Harris from Forest Hill in South London. In the late 1970s the Mk1 Capri became the most popular car in Spedeworth's 3-litre hot rod formula called 'super rods'.

Sometimes it seemed like the phrases 'Wimbledon hot rods' and 'rain' were used together a great deal. The October BP Supernationals at Wimbledon were certainly contested in very wet conditions. Derek Green (6) and Paul Smyth (64) are seen here lining up with the other red tops for what is going to be a difficult race.

Ever the showman, Barry Lee even made it onto the front cover of *Custom Car* magazine in the company of a topless model. The session took place at Walthamstow Stadium, with Leapy eventually being photographed in his undies while 'Naughty Nicola' modelled his gold lamé overalls!

two

# 1974–1976

Ex-rallycross man John Geeves made a big impression on the formula in 1974 with this smart Mini.

Dave Bozzard was a star driver for many years and one of the few to secure the silver roof of the national points leader. Rather than displaying the traditional roof fin, this 1974 model sported a unique restyling with which to sport his racing number.

George Polley made a return to racing in 1974 in this smart Mk1 Escort, his third season in the colours of BP/*Custom Car*. He was soon to return to his beloved Ford Anglia, however.

Alan Burtenshaw's neat Ford Anglia in action on his only ever visit to White City in 1974. The Sussex-based man was a versatile and successful racer – a double champion (National and British) in bangers in 1976 and a front-runner in stock rods. The Escort (169) is Malcolm Springham from Harlow.

Trackstar promotion action from 1974. Tommy Gillon (50) spins, causing Bill Mayers (22) to take evasive action at Kirkby. Mayers was the points champion at Doncaster raceway in 1974.

Tommy Upton's 1600cc Mk3 Cortina leads Mal Edge off the banking at New Brighton. The Liverpool circuit opened for business in 1969 and staged some great racing. The circuit was unique for having very steep banking.

Cortina time as Jim Foote's Mk1 leads Pete Helms' Mk2. Helms was part of the New Brighton team who stunned the 'stars' from Hednesford by beating them in a team match by 33 points to 22 in 1975.

Pete Helms aims his Cortina up the inside of Tommy Gillon.

Two quick Hednesford Mini men from 1974. They are Alan Timms (37) – a Midlands regular in the first half of the 1970s and part of the massive Kenilworth Autos team that ran 4/6 cars ranging from 100E through to Minis, Anglias and Escorts – and Barry Owens (11) from Southport.

Hednesford man Duncan Sawey (41) leads an impressive Mini/Anglia battle in 1974.

Keith Green from Tipton in the West Midlands competed in hot rods for a couple of years and was a consistent Blue Grader. He is pictured in the pit area at Hednesford.

Kenny Ireland was one of the first hot rod superstars north of the border and a former Scottish Champion in the superstox and stock car formulas. He was third in the 1974 British Championship and gave the established stars a scare in the early stages of the World Championship in the same year.

Trevor Redmond's *Autospeed* organization staged a one-off meeting at Wembley featuring cars from all the leading promoters. Ex-autocross and rallycross man Don Gilham is seen here at speed in what was the most famous stadium in the country. Gilham was a very able driver who always presented a nice-looking car. He now lives in New Zealand and still has the occasional race in Minis.

The 1974 World Championship was the first one to include drivers from Holland, Germany and Belgium. Ike van der Wal, the Dutchman who had previously raced superstox, dices here with German driver Heinz Gobbels.

Cyril Wilcox looks happy after a win at Hednesford. Even in the early 1970s Wilcox, from Market Drayton, was a veteran of the class with nearly ten years under his belt. Wins like this meant that he was well qualified to represent the Midlands at the 1974 World Championship. Below, he is seen dicing with the American representative, Bud Gail (132).

Les Kay (above) normally raced under number 64 but switched to number 4 in the World Championship due a clash with Paul Smyth (below). The change of number did no harm to his luck, as he took fourth place. A national numbering system was still five years away at this point. Kay was the first Scot to win races in the three classes north of the border (stock saloons, superstox and hot rods). In hot rods he won the Scottish Championship in 1973 and was points champion in 1974.

The Imp was one of the most popular cars in Scotland. John 'The Captain' Kirk was one of the drivers responsible for its success. He started hot rod racing in 1971 and was runner up in the Scottish Points Championship in 1972 and 1973. He quit hot rods to return to the circuits in 1974 after a torrid time when he wrote off two cars in quick succession.

Action from the 1974 World Championship. Midland ace Brian Vawer's Mini splashes through a huge puddle on the inside. John Geeves (177) is trying to get away, although Barry Lee is using the outside line to progress towards his second title.

Leon Smith signals his retirement from the 1974 World Championship. Mick Collard's second livery of the season was that of Yately Commercial Motors.

German star Josef Volkenstein's last season (1974) in a VW Beetle (complete with Mercedes grille). He switched to an NSU for 1975.

Ex-speedway rider Tony Marren's smart Escort.

Danish butcher-turned-racer Poul Pedersen bought this smart Escort over to race in 1974. The Danish drivers used rallycross cars, which ran to a similar specification to UK hot rods.

If you hadn't realized from the other pictures, the 1974 World Championship final was a little on the wet side, as can be seen from this post-race picture of Mick Collard.

*Opposite above:* Barry Lee became the first driver to successfully defend the World Championship when he won the 1974 event. Here he is interviewed after the event by popular race commentator John Earrey. Sadly, John died while this book was being collated.

*Opposite below:* Barry Lee's crew get to work changing a wheel and a spark plug in the mandatory pit stop in the first ever Grand Prix at Wimbledon on 9 November 1974. The races featured a Le Mans start (with drivers running to their cars). Dave Bozzard took the win, with Martin Freestone's crew setting the fastest time in the pit stops.

GOODYEAR

01-553-1614
ROD ON

Spedeworth expanded their promotions onto the grass tracks at Great Chart (near Ashford in Kent) and Billingshurst (near Horsham in Sussex) in 1975. These ventures were popular with race fans but less so with the local authorities and residents. As a result, this form of racing was short lived. Waiting for the off at Billingshurst are James Smith (414) and Pete Winstone (128).

Camberley man Bert Arnell races on his home track, Aldershot, in early 1975. It looks like ideal conditions for a Mini too.

Our first look at Ulster hot rodding. The formula started in Ulster in 1975 and Richard Turtle was one of the first to race there with this VW Beetle, pictured here at Aghadowey. The Cullybackey man eventually swapped the VW for an Anglia before progressing on to the ubiquitous Escort.

Sonny Howard's unique Datsun 1200 Coupé debuted in 1975. This was the first of literally hundreds of cars from Sonny, who became the sport's most prolific car builder. The Glovers of Ely team started in rallying before running a parallel campaign on the ovals. Sonny took the car to three wins in his first three race meetings! Jeff Cushing is the driver of the Escort (75) on the outside line.

*Opposite above:* Wimbledon-domiciled Italian driver Salvo Falcone is a long-serving and popular racer. So popular in fact that some fans once lobbied the organizers to allow him to represent Italy in the World Championship! They were not successful. Salvo has always put his family and business first and therefore based the majority of his racing at Wimbledon Stadium, just a short distance from his bakery. This shot, however, captures him on an outing at Arlington raceway.

*Opposite below:* The Grand Parade at Aldershot in 1975. Kingston-based Martin Robertson (90) also raced in Grand Prix Midgets with ex-Formula One driver Paul Emery's team. The Ford Anglia (104) belongs to Sutton's Chris Carter, while the 37 is Micky Elliott who was one of the last star Mini drivers.

179
SALVO
179

37
90

A look at the grid for the 1975 World Championship. Brian Pedley drew pole position with Dutchman Kees Grashoff alongside and Les Trussler and Bruce Peacock on row two.

John Edwards lines up ready for the 1975 World Championship. Outside him is the 1974 Scottish Champion Davy Philp. Both men were to make successful transitions to the big circuits – Edwards in various saloon car classes and Philp in eurocar and pickups.

Brian Pedley led the race for some time until an oil leak caused the clutch to slip. However, he did have the consolation of winning one of the support races which was televised by ITV's *World of Sport* programme.

Guildford-based Les 'Tramp' Trussler was a star driver for a short while, even qualifying for the 1975 World Championship.

4
REVOLUTION WHEELS
YATELEY COMMERCIAL MOTORS
4

H 108
BURTON
VULCAN
H 1
563

*Above:* Midlands ace John Edwards (112) dices with defending Champion Barry Lee (351) in the 1975 World Championship at Ipswich. Lee's car, the only Mk2 Escort in the field, sported a white and gold livery to match the gold roof that he'd won the previous two seasons. Lee finished second after being drawn at the back of the grid, while Edwards was a creditable sixth.

*Opposite above:* Colourful South African racer Johan Coetzee borrowed a car from Mick Collard for the 1975 Championship.

*Opposite below:* German Champion Wolfgang Vohs' NSU engages in battle with Micky Hall (563) and Bob Howe (108).

Hednesford mêlée in early September 1975, with Trevor Shaw (23) seemingly heading fencewards. Cyril Wilcox's new Escort (219) makes contact with Bob Hedges (119).

Consistent front-runner Bryan Wright in his Anglia at Ipswich during the 1975 World Championship where he achieved his best ever result of third place behind Derek Fiske and Barry Lee. Wright was also the London Champion in 1975.

Ted Allan went through the grades very quickly. He started with the Honda S800, pictured here with a white roof at Wimbledon. As he moved through the grades he moved on to more conventional machinery, first an Anglia, then a Mk2 Escort and finally the first Talbot Sunbeam.

Four years on from winning the formula's first World Championship, Bob Howe still prepares an immaculate car, pictured here at Wimbledon in 1976.

Mike Bennett arrives early for a 1976 meeting at Wimbledon. Kent-based racer Bennett was a Blue Graded driver at the time – no mean feat in a year when Spedeworth had so many cars racing that they had to run separate heats for the White Grade.

Londoner Micky Hall with his Escort in the pit area at Wimbledon in 1976.

Top Midlands racers Jon Brookes and Stuart Jackson showed just how competitive the Mini was on the UK's fastest quarter-mile oval, Hednesford raceway. Both men eventually made the switch to Escorts.

Frank Hartley's unique Blimp (short for British Leyland Imp), which had a 1340cc Mini engine and front subframe bolted in the back. Frank built two versions of the Blimp, the first of which was written off at Ipswich after going flat out into the wall (Frank seems to have had an affinity with the Foxhall wall).

CEWAY
D & W TYRES
202
ADAMS & BLAND
3

H
238
MOTOR.
INSURANCE
56

Midlands racer Neil Clarke has raced in each of the last five decades starting with economy cars at Hednesford in the 1960s. His hot rod days saw him get through several Minis. He then moved on to super rods, stock rods and then Grand Prix Midgets.

*Above:* Excitement at Hednesford as Paul Grimer spins his Mini. Peter Bache's Holbay-powered Anglia (13) is already safe on the inside and John Edwards (Mini 112) looks like he'll squeeze past on the outside. Merseysider Pete Helms (2) follows up.

*Previous spread:* A big moment at Hednesford in 1976 for Gordon Bland (356), Neil Clarke (202) and Tom Laffey (background, being pushed away). Many consider this shunt to have scuppered Laffey's World Championship hopes that year, although he still took second place to George Polley. The Avenger (238) is driven by Pete Rogerson. There are also several Capris on circuit – the fledgling 'Late Model Speedcar' class ran with the hot rods until there were enough of them to run races on their own.

Bob Sharp (91) engages with Peter Bache (Anglia) with John Edwards (112) hot on their heels at Hednesford. Bache was soon to retire from the sport while Sharp became one of the early stars of the new super rod formula.

Top Mini racer Paul Grimer (8) was later to switch to a Ford Escort. His pursuer here, Trevor Shaw (23), had already made the switch.

504
TERRY SELBY
RED COW RACING TEAM
504
140
BRIDGE INN" RACING TEAM
140

563
S S DEVELOPMENTS
16
16
48

*Above:* Large roof wings are more associated with Formula One and Two stock cars from the late 1980s onwards. This one was sported by the flamboyant South African driver Johan Coetzee.

*Opposite above:* Scottish ace Graham Wait (140) raced hot rods from the age of seventeen and used the Hillman Imp initially for a number of years before switching to the more conventional Escort. Here he dices with London-based racer Terry Selby, who was only on the scene for a short while.

*Opposite below:* Karli Heuhsen's smart NSU lines up ready for the 1976 World Championship. To his outside are Londoner Micky Hall (563) and Dutchman Ger Verstegen (48). The continental drivers' left-hand drive cars were rarely competitive on the UK tracks, but drivers like Heuhsen could be unbeatable on home circuits like Kaldenkirchen in Germany.

Tom Laffey awaits the off in the 1976 World Championship. The Midlands ace drew pole position with Dane Arnold Larsen alongside. Bill McLellan (left) and Micky Codling (right) form the second row. 1972 champ Bob Howe is on the third row with Pete Stevens on his outside.

Carl Erik Kristensen pictured in the 1976 World Championship final dicing with Barry Lee. This was the Dane's last appearance in the World Championship but he used the car, a borrowed Ford Anglia, to compete in an England *v.* Europe test series. The car was unfortunately written off in a huge pile-up in the test match at Great Yarmouth.

Northern Ireland were to become a major force in hot rod racing in later years. The Ulster lads first contested the World Championship final in 1976 with Robert Francey (10) seen here dicing with Micky Codling (566). Future Ballymena co-promoter Ernie Kilpatrick also represented them.

South African racer Corry Sammons bought over his own Ford Anglia for the World Championship in 1976. Corry began racing in 1972 and was first selected to race for the South African team that beat the UK in 1973. Corry was the top points scorer in that series.

Not many drivers can claim to have won major titles in two different short-circuit formulae. Diss-based Derek Fiske was a three times British Champion in superstox before moving into hot rods where he won the 1975 World Championship.

Aubrey 'Foxy' Dance was already a hugely popular driver in stock saloons before moving into hot rods. He is seen here dicing with George Polley at the 1976 Spedeweekend. Sadly Foxy passed away in 2003 but his memory lives on as his son Rob is a star driver and races in today's 2-litre formula complete with the fox mascot on the roof of his car.

An overseas trio in action at Ipswich. Dutchman Cees De Haas chases down the inside of South African Jan du Plessis, while Ulster driver Ernie Kilpatrick's Mini (155) is eclipsed on the outside line.

George Polley on his way to winning the 1976 World Championship. The purple Ford Anglia was very much the Polley trademark – indeed, he was the only driver to win the World Championship in the model.

In the 1976 World Championship race, defending champion Derek Fiske is eclipsed by a driver who would take the title three years later, Gordon Bland.

Phil Powell (331) made it to the 1976 World Championship, his days as 'mechanic to George Polley' well behind him and a star driver in his own right. Phil is dicing with Duffy Collard (19, outside) and Johan Coetzee (4). This was Collard's debut in the Mk2 Escort after he wrote off his Mk1 'testing' it on his farm!

1976 was renowned as a long, hot summer but somehow the terms 'hot rods' and 'August bank holiday' meant the first rain for months! Ez Walker's Anglia awaits the off at Hednesford.

Barry Lee in the pits at Wimbledon on 14 August 1976 after a photo shoot for *Autosport* magazine. The magazine carried reports on the sport's major events for a short while.

George Polley on his double lap of honour after winning the 1976 World Championship at Ipswich.

three

# 1977–1979

134
Musical
Equipment from
134
BP
HASTINGS SOUND

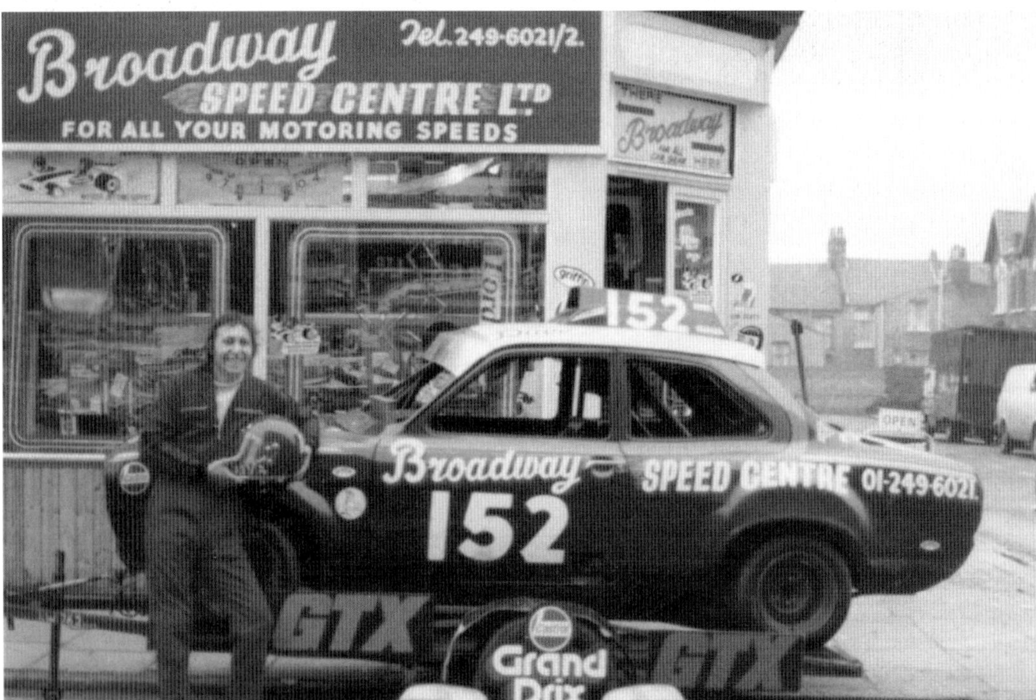
Broadway
Tel. 249-6021/2.
SPEED CENTRE LTD
FOR ALL YOUR MOTORING SPEEDS
152
Broadway
SPEED CENTRE 01-249-6021
152
GTX
Grand Prix
GTX

*Above:* Nevin 'Sticky' Torrens was the first Northern Irish hot rod star. He won the 1975 and 1976 Irish Championship races and was points champion. He also won the first ever Open Championship in 1976. For 1977 he picked up sponsorship from the Causeway Safari Park and sported this striking zebra livery.

*Opposite above:* By 1977 Hastings man Jerry Wilson was climbing the ranks with an effective Mk1 Escort, pictured here at Wimbledon.

*Opposite below:* Dave Hitchen arrived on the national scene in 1977 with this smart Mk1 Escort backed by Broadway Speed Centre. He soon made it to Red Grade and stayed there until his retirement when he went back to grass-track racing. Dave has made a comeback to hot rods during the last couple of years.

Terry Soper made Red Grade with the *Autospeed* promotion using this rapid Mini Pick-up. This photograph was taken in the pit area at Newton Abbot. The Pick-up may appear unconventional, but the West Country 'Production Car' formula, from which hot rods evolved, included such vehicles in its early days.

This great-looking Mk1 Volkswagen Golf was driven by the German star Josef Thissen in the 1977 World Championship at Ipswich.

Northern Ireland were represented at the 1977 World Championships by the Jackson brothers, Derek (3, above) and Alastair (26, below). Alastair was widely tipped to be the man to upset the English stranglehold on the formula after making the English superstox look rather silly in a meeting at Wimbledon where he lapped the entire field.

*Above:* Barry Lee shows the rest of the field a clean pair of heels in the 1977 World Championship as he heads towards his third title.

*Below:* Barry with the spoils of victory. The gold and silver overalls have now made way for black, studded flares!

Gordon Bland picks up the 1977 Irish Open Championship trophy at Aghadowey. He is flanked by runners up Leslie Dallas (left) and Alistair Jackson (right).

A Wimbledon dice between Ted Allan (114), who had now moved on to the Ford Anglia, and Salvo Falcone (179), who was now Escort-mounted.

*Above:* The Spedeworth promotion often found an excuse for some exciting team racing. First it was against the Danes, next the Hednesford promotion and then the rallycross boys. Here we see Micky Hall's '*Starsky and Hutch*'-liveried Escort being hurled across the grass at Paddock Hill, Brands Hatch on an 'away' encounter.

*Opposite above:* Salvo Falcone (179), Derek Wileman (99), Roy Cook (110) and Bob Saill (55) await the off at Arlington.

*Opposite below:* Barry Lee was the first man to race the Mk1 and Mk2 Escorts in hot rods and was tipped to be the first to race 'Ford's New Baby', the Fiesta. In actual fact it was Jeff Ditchman who was the first (and one of the few) to race the model. The car was not a success and ultimately found its way over the water to Northern Ireland. The later model Fiesta was to become a popular shape for hot rod racing when the formula began to use space frames. After the Fiesta experiment Ditchman quit the formula and raced with a little more success in super rods.

110
BP
179
99
55

EXCHANGE
GEARBOXES
520 8386 · 520 5275
E
SCHREIDER
25

Pete Winstone's smart Escort Mk2 in the pit area at Aldershot Stadium early in 1978. Winstone emulated Barry Lee's feat of winning the European Championship two years in succession in 1976 and 1977. The European Champion's roof chequer can be seen on the car.

Surrey driver Chris Gautrey made the successful switch from stock saloons to hot rods. Unusually he used an MGB engine for most of his hot rod career and was always one to watch in the wet. Chris is pictured here about to participate in a Grand Parade at Aldershot.

Mike Meade was a short-lived star on the Spedeworth raceways with this immaculate Ford Escort. Meade is still out and about racing nearly thirty years later on the big circuits in 750 Motor Club events.

Roger Tanner's smart Mini ready for action in the pits at Aldershot Stadium. Roger was to attain Blue Grade with this car.

The only Mick Collard Mk2 Escort to sport the RS-style droop snoot.

Ulsterman 'Sticky' Torrens converted his Avenger rally car to hot rod specification prior to building the first Talbot-powered Sunbeam. He is pictured in action at Ballymena, although the crowd's attention seems to be elsewhere!

Jo Clerx represented Holland in the 'World Best Pairs' competition at Wimbledon on 19 August 1978. Wim Haagen in his unusual Fiat 124 (below) was half of the Belgian pairing. Sadly, the Europeans were outclassed at this meeting, with only the Scottish drivers presenting any challenge to the English pair of Lee and Collard.

*Above:* Ormond Christie is best remembered for racing the Toyota Starlet, but came to prominence with the Triumph Spitfire with which he won the 1978 British Championship at Cowdenbeath. Ormond was not the first driver to race a Spitfire as a hot rod – superstox star Dave Pierce had used the model on a brief sabbatical from the contact formula due to a bad back. Hot rods derived from sports cars were outlawed shortly after Christie's title win.

*Opposite above:* Barry Lee is congratulated by the sponsor of second-place Jon Brookes after his fourth World Championship win at Ipswich in 1978. The scene also shows the car of Paul Grimer (8) in the foreground with Brian Wright (left) checking under the bonnet of his Ford Anglia. The Escort in the background (centre) belongs to German ace Rolf Arens, while the Escort on the right of the shot is that of Scotsman Kenny Ireland.

*Opposite below:* Barry Lee waves to the crowd after his win. Also on the podium are Les Eaton (with arms by his sides), *Custom Car* magazine's Colin Gamm and race commentator John Earrey.

8

BURTON
FAMILY HOLIDAY
DUFFY HR19
SPEDEWORTH

Betty Shaw was the only lady racer in the inaugural hot rod Grand Prix Series. Representing Skegness Stadium, her smart Mini is pictured in the pits at Wimbledon Stadium in a visit to gain some practice prior to the final round of the 1978 series. Betty was a very successful driver and won the Midland Roadshows British Championship in 1977.

Bill Pennycook's Mini finds itself in the wall at Ipswich in one of the support races for the 1978 Spedeweekend.

Mick Keen (197) awaits the off with Tim Staple (107) at Ipswich in 1978.

Jerry Wilson continued to improve and impress but could have achieved a lot more from his racing. He ultimately received backing from BP Oils but was perhaps a victim of the sport's progression, as national competition became more important than strong local performances. He did, however, finish third in the 1978 World Championship.

John Duhig (406) often troubled the regular star-graded drivers and is seen here battling with Duffy Collard (19) and Barry Lee at Wimbledon in 1978. John was not able to race regularly owing to work commitments in Saudi Arabia. He now lives in the United States.

Chelmsford racer Lloyd Shelley is still actively involved in motor sports, albeit on a local level. He set the Spedeworth circuits alight first as a novice in a Mini and then with an Anglia and then finally with this neat Escort Mk1.

Stuart Maidment represented the West Country promoter Autospeed in the inaugural Grand Prix Series. The Cullompton-based driver was a mechanic by profession and graduated to hot rods after racing bangers for three seasons. Stuart was one of the top racers in the region and won the Cornish Championship in 1978.

Ted Allan was the first man to race a Talbot Sunbeam in hot rods, albeit with Ford power. His car is pictured here in the pit area at Arlington Stadium in 1978.

South London driver Dave Thompson made it to Star Grade as an Anglia driver but maintained that status with this Mk1 Escort.

The 1977 English Champion Colin Facey at Wimbledon in 1978. Colin came to hot rods from autocross racing and raced an Opel Kadett with limited success in 1976, before switching to the more conventional Escort shown here.

One of the last quick Mini men was Greenford's Micky Elliott.

The late 1970s saw the arrival of a quick teenage driver by the name of Paul Knight. He had all the right equipment, including an ex-Barry Lee car, but never scored in major championships.

Paul Knight RACING
65

78
Mervyn Percy

*Above:* Midland ace Jon Brookes on a rare outing at Wimbledon Stadium, most likely for the final round of the 1978 Grand Prix Series. The London venue used a variety of methods for separating the inner, shale speedway circuit from the outer, tarmac stock car track. The solution here was a length of tyres joined together, but they were unfortunately quite easily deranged.

*Opposite above:* Paul Knight's previously immaculate Escort found itself in need of some TLC after a racing incident at Ipswich. The Andrews of Ealing team always prepared a neat car and would no doubt have been back on duty within a matter of days.

*Opposite below:* The first Ulsterman to win a race in England was young Tyrrell Arnold, who won a support race at the 1979 European Championship meeting at Hednesford in his three-day-old Mini. Tyrrell is pictured here in the pit area at Portadown.

Hot rod racing was becoming a proper national sport, with all the promoters running to standard rules and all affording their drivers the chance to race against those from other organizations. Spedeworth's Hot Rod Picnic meeting at Ringwood was probably the biggest-ever gathering of the cars. This is PRI's Stan Vile on the Grand Parade with his immaculate Mk1 Escort.

The lap of honour following the final round of the inaugural hot rod Grand Prix Series. Barry Lee (back right, with chequered flag) won the series, but the Spedeworth Control Car is weighed down with his two mechanics on the bonnet plus 'the father of hot rod racing', Bill Morris (left, at the back of the car). Between Bill and Barry is the man who took a surprise win in that final round, Bovingdon racer Dave 'Moony' McMahon.

Barry Lee became the first works hot rod driver and drove the Dealer Opel Team Kadett GTE for the first part of the season. The partnership however, which extended to his rallycross programme as well, was not a success and he was back in a Ford Escort in the summer.

National numbering is now in evidence in some parts of the UK, with the West Country drivers getting the 700s. Frank Turner always turned out a smart car, as evidenced by this shot of his Mk1 Escort in the pit area at Newton Abbot. Just behind Frank's car is Merv Hutching's banger – Merv was himself an able hot rod driver.

Ken Salter from Cullompton in Devon represented *Autospeed* in the 1978 Grand Prix Series. As an ex-professional footballer and judo champion he was used to serious competition (and I dare say no one picked a fight with him either).

Ralph Sanders was a regular representative for *Autospeed*. A garage owner from Exeter, he was a successful driver who won the Grand Prix of Devon in the 1970s. He went on to win the English Championship in the 1980s.

Bob Bickers' Anglia pictured in the pits at Newton Abbot. Of course, there is always an exception to the rule and for some reason Bob did not adopt the West Country national numbering convention. He represented the *Autospeed* promotion in the 1979 Grand Prix Series.

Sussex man Graham Kircher was a top driver in stock saloons and then stock rods but never quite made it to the very top in hot rods despite taking wins in this unusual car in 1979. The Mazda RX3 was powered not by the conventional Ford or even an MGB engine, but by an 1800cc Volvo lump.

187
144
144

*Above:* Daventry man Trevor Shaw joined the sport in 1972 and, like many top Midlands drivers, progressed from Mini to Escort. This model took him to the runner-up spot in the 1979 World Championship behind Gordon Bland. After quitting hot rods he raced successfully on the long circuits in single-seaters. Sadly Trevor passed away while this book was being collated.

*Opposite above:* David Oates in action at Ipswich, dicing with Tommy Field. Oates went on to drive in several formulae both on the ovals and on the long circuits, always with exceptionally well-presented cars. He also won the Willhire 24-hour saloon car race with fellow ex-oval racers Roy Eaton and Gordon Lauder.

*Opposite below:* In its second season the Grand Prix Series extended its geographical boundary and visited Northern Ireland. Ormond Christie won the Aghadowey round with Jerry Wilson (left) and Pete Stevens (right) third and second respectively.

121
H 121
BP

5
LESLIE DALLAS
5
BP

*Above:* Early laps of the 1979 World Championship. Leon Smith (401) is the first car in picture and is leading this group featuring (from left to right) Ted Allan (114), Duffy Collard (19), Gordon Bland (356) and Ormond Christie (62). Gordon went on to win the race but was denied his fifteen minutes of fame as the normally televised event fell victim to a strike at ITV. This was the last World Championship race to feature a ballot for grid positions.

*Opposite above:* Ex-kart racer Ken Churchill was noted for bringing the brand name of Colman's Mustard into the sport. It remains probably the biggest brand name to be promoted in the class. The Camberley man started in the sport with a Mk1 Escort and progressed to this RS-fronted Mk2 after reaching Star status.

*Opposite below:* The late Leslie Dallas became one of the top Ulster hot rod racers racing the famous 'Cookstown Sizzler' Escorts. This is an early photograph of him racing a Mini at the 1979 Spedeweekend.

*Above:* Ormond Christie's bid for the 1979 World Championship ended with damage to his Triumph Herald. He was to wait another two years before taking the title.

*Opposite above:* The hot rod Grand Prix Series added a round at Brands Hatch for the 1979 series – the race taking place on the Clearways Oval. Jim Mensley's unusual Toyota is in the paddock at this event. Tom Laffey's immaculate Chevrolet Camaro ASCAR racer is just behind.

*Opposite below:* Rod Birley's Talbot Sunbeam ready for action at Brands Hatch. Rod was a front-runner for the PRI and Northampton promotions before returning to the big circuits. He is still an active driver and does a great deal behind the scenes to bring long- and short-circuit disciplines together in special team events.

COMPOMOTIVE WHEELS
18

PROTO
ROD BIRLEY
PROTO
44

Photocall prior to the 1979 Irish Open Championship final at Aghadowey. From left to right, back row: Jim Barclay, Leslie Dallas, Roy Cook, Keith Newman, Stuart Jackson, Ian Bruce, Sticky Torrens, Peter Grimer, Barry Lee, Kenny Ireland, Ormond Christie, Pete Stevens, Gordon Bland. Front row: Danny Butler, Bertie McCrory, Kevin Tierney, Richard Turtle, Paul Grimer, Adrian Kirkland, Stevie Morrison.

After his spell with Dealer Opel Team, Barry Lee was soon back in a Ford Escort. He is pictured here in practice for the 1979 Irish Open Championship at Aghadowey.

Roberta Hamilton presents Barry Lee with the 1979 Irish Open Championship trophy. Former champion Gordon Bland (right) was second, with Peter Grimer (left) third. This was Lee's last visit to Northern Ireland for some time.

A cosmopolitan line-up at Hednesford for the 1979 European Championship, including Peter Schmitz (45), Paul van den Broek (10), Kenny Ireland (196), Cees De Haas (21) and Bernie Diment (186).